Now What??

Toni Cowart

ISBN: 978-0-9912402-6-5

SunShack is an imprint of Southern and Unshackled Ministries,
LLC.

Credits:

Editors: Gwynn Schneider

DEDICATION

For Tess
My cousin, my kinfolk, but most of all, my sister in Christ. You are a
shining example, who has shown not only myself, but countless
others, what grace under fire looks like. Thank you for being a light
in a dark world.

CONTENTS

IMPORTANT NOTE

Please note: In this book, it is on purpose that the words- satan, enemy, evil one, master manipulator or any other words used to refer to "the thief" who comes to steal, kill and destroy, are not capitalized. I will not give him the uppercase value.

~ ACKNOWLEDGEMENTS ~

I want to thank all the ladies who allowed me an interview with you. You allowed me a glimpse into where you've been and who you are. The who you are that the outside world doesn't always get to see. I've seen glimpses of your struggles, heartaches and triumphs. Through talking and listening with each of you I've seen brave and courageous women who have kept on keepin' on — even when they thought nothing was left to give. Many of you stood and fought and then, when you thought you had nothing left, you fought some more. You are my heroes and you are leaving a legacy for others to follow. Keep up the good fight ladies and remember Who fights for you.

1
NOW WHAT ??

If you are looking for fluff – this book is not for you. This is a book for those willing to sweep the fluff away and get down to business. This book is not for the faint of heart, but neither is life.

Have you ever wished you could know what lay ahead? Or, that you could prepare for the unimaginable? Maybe you've even found yourself saying, "Now what?".

We don't always know what is around the corner and more often than not, we feel ill equipped to handle many adverse situations, when they do come calling. Truth be told, alone, we are ill equipped to handle many of them.

Good news! – you are not the first person to find yourself wondering these things, much less, asking "Now what?" when finding yourself in the midst of a storm or facing a new season of life.

Whatever is around the corner, whatever you feel may be unbearable – is not. It may be humanly impossible to bear, BUT – enter Jesus.

Speaking of Jesus, if you have ever been told that you need Jesus so you will go to heaven, well, this is correct. Yes, salvation means eternity in heaven instead of hell, BUT it also means so much more. The "so much more" is what I am so eager to share with you.

An intimate relationship with Jesus means ~ Peace (supernatural peace) ~ Discernment ~ Knowledge (heart knowledge) ~ Life more abundant ~ Sound mind ~ Joy ~ Love ~ Hope ~ Understanding your Worth ~ Having A powerful weapon to combat evil in this world. ~ Etc.

I don't know of one person that would not love to have one or all in the above list. All of the above is possible, and if you want to know the truth, I am not sure I could function on a daily basis without the peace and hope that I have from my Jesus.

Have you ever been to the beach and stood with your toes in the edge of the water? If you stand there for very long the water comes up and washes sand out from under your feet, making it hard to continue to stand. Well, life is like that sometimes.

Sometimes you just need to be able to "stand". With Jesus you will be able to stand, your knees may quiver and the waves may come, but even when the sand is swept away from under your feet, you will still be standing. That is what spending time with Jesus will do for you.

I recently ran across something that I would love to share with you. I wrote this back in 2014 while doing a Bible study. In the Bible study we were asked "What does the Bible mean to you?" My answer stirred up so many things within myself, one of which was further igniting my passion of sharing Jesus so others may experience all He has to offer.

Here is what I wrote as the answer to, what does the Bible mean to me:

> For me it's a tangible, yet still supernatural, hands and "eyes on" with my Lord. It's a part of Him (and since He's a part of me) it is now a part of me too. It's a preciousness of our relationship. I don't have to have a copy of the Bible to have that relationship with Him and yet I'd want it no other way! Every time I open His Word it's as though I feel His breath, the very breath that first breathed the Word into existence, has just breathed on me. And oh, how sweet that is.

So often I feel He shows me something new in His Word. It's as though I'm holding a mystery book that's just between Him & me (like a secret) that if I'll open it, He'll whisper new secrets into my heart that He's already died to share.

I have however learned, He doesn't want me to keep these secrets to myself. I am to share with every one of you who will bear with me. I will share Jesus until I breath my last breath.

Full disclaimer though - As Paul says in (*1 Corinthians 2:1-2*)

> "*...I don't come with excellence of speech or wisdom declaring to you the testimony of God. 2/ For I am determined to know nothing among you except Jesus Christ and Him crucified.*"

Folks, I know that this is not an eloquent book of words but my prayer is that it will reflect Jesus and will leave you wanting more of the "so much more" of a life with Jesus.

2
SEASONS

Seasons change ~ and so do we

Let's talk about seasons for a moment. Seasons come and go. I am not just talking about the four seasons we know as spring, summer, fall and winter. I am talking about the seasons of our lives and sometimes, the seasons of our hearts.

As these seasons come and go, make no mistake, with each new season is a chance to make a difference, start again, or pick up and carry on with your head held high; and we are never too old nor is it too late to begin a new season.

Many of our seasons, current or new, seem to be sprinkled with "I am" statements. Or at least the circumstance that catapulted us to begin a new journey often begins with "I am".

We need to remember, and be very mindful, that as we walk through our day, we are surrounded by people with these burdensome "I am" statements. We may pass them at the post office, the grocery store or even sit beside them in church; they may very well be the one taking our order at the restaurant. We all have "I am" statements, and some are painful.

When I embarked on this book for women, I knew immediately, that I would need to talk to other women. So, I did just that. I set out to interview many women of all ages and walks of life. My youngest to interview has been 19 and the oldest is 82. I wanted to hear straight from them, where they've been and what all went in to molding them into the women they are today.

I wanted to hear about their struggles and their triumphs, their heart breaks and their joys. These are the things that made shoulders sag, hearts smile, and those tears that would not stop, and somewhere along the way, strengthened our backbone; ultimately making us who we are today.

Here are the "I am" statements from some of the ladies I interviewed. A couple are my own.

I am...
~I am a young mom in the throes of changing diapers, wiping noses, butts and mouths (not necessarily in that order) while cleaning, and cooking. There is that

ever-prolific pile of laundry that multiplies before I can say, "now what"? All the while just trying to make it until the end of day and then collapse in bed already three days tired and it is only Monday. Now what?

~I am wearing these long sleeves because I have bruises. My bruising goes deeper than my skin. My heart is covered with them. Who knew, verbal abuse and mental abuse cut so deep. Now what?

~I am so confused! My son just informed us he is gay. How can that be? Now what?

~After twenty-five years of marriage my spouse says he doesn't love me anymore. So, now what?

~My daughter just denounced Jesus and is claiming agnosticism. But we raised her in a Christian home?!

~I am busy trying to juggle both a career and a family with young children who all have activities. Oh, and somewhere in there is a husband – can't neglect him. Tired is the one word that I completely feel at one with.

~I just walked into church or another function, smiling and greeting everyone when just moments before I had been yelled at, belittled and degraded. Out of habit I respond with a smile and say, "I'm good, and you?"

~I am just being handed my long awaited new born and am told, "He has special needs and we will send someone in to tell you more about his condition". My heart is already defending our new bundle and my emotions are already feeling the weariness of future battles that haven't even begun yet. Now what?

~I am carrying guilt and shame for things that happened many years ago, when I was a child. Things I had no control over. Some predator saw his target and took advantage. I carry those terrifying memories that haunt me no matter how many years it has been.

~I am now divorced. I didn't get married to get divorced. Yet, here I stand holding the papers that declare me just that. I feel the stares and hear the whispers, even at church. I try to hold my head up high while my insides are crying out. Now what?

~I am bebopping through life when I begin to hear murmurings of a virus. Within next two weeks the murmurings increase and certain travel is banned. Boom, along with the whole country I am now in a "state of quarantine". I find myself standing and gaping at empty shelves while mumbling, "I've never seen anything like this in my lifetime". Now what?

~ I am a recovering addict. People still murmur about my past, even though it is my past. I have come so far, but, now what?

~I am burying my 6, 8 and 10-year-old children after they were killed by a drunk driver in an automobile accident. To say my world has just been rocked is an understatement. Now what?

~I have just returned home from serving my country, now what?

~I am trying to make it through chemo.

~I am a new graduate and will begin college this fall. But the unimaginable happens first, now what?

~I am newly retired, now what?

~I am in a brand-new season of my life, now what?

~I am facing my husband's cancer diagnoses and not sure what tomorrow will look like for us, for me. Now what?

~I am 82 and honestly, I never thought I'd live this long. I am thankful, but - Now what?

      Whatever your "I am" statement is, if you find yourself asking that "now what" question – hold on and dig in because this book is just for you.

~~ This space is for you to write your current "I am" statement ~~

_____

_____

_____

_____

_____

_____

_____

_____

_____

_____

We will have more "new seasons" in our lives than we would have ever figured! Seasons weather us. This can be a good thing, if, we can learn to embrace these seasons.

Embracing a season doesn't necessarily mean we like it. It means we didn't hide our head in the sand, we didn't crawl in a closet hoping when we emerged that life had carried on and passed what we were hiding from. It means we dealt with it while putting one foot in front of the other.

Women can be exceptional at doing what needs to be done. I believe God knew this would be one of the incredible ways we would be a helper to our husband and often in spite of circumstances. Let's take Mary for instance. Mary, as in the mother of Jesus.

In Luke 2 Mary is pregnant, as in the last trimester pregnant, and of course, it is time for the

Census. So off they trek. She's heavy with child, el' prego, bout to bust, feels like a beached whale. Yet, she must perch herself on a donkey and ride, ride, ride.

Then, labor begins and there is not a Holiday Inn in sight. Seriously, there is nothing comfortable or nice with available room for her, and the labor pains persist. But, there's a barn! Barns come with critters both big and small. (I've been a farm girl so I can so easily picture this, small critters mean mice, I don't like mice!) Large animals, hay, and manure, the whole shebang.

Mary does what she must. Her body pays not attention to where she is and the pains continue as they press and squeeze the little Lord Jesus into this world. She gives birth. She gives birth in the very "last resort" of circumstances. The Messiah is born. She is now finally able to hold this child she has carried and felt move within her. She is able to watch His little arms and legs move with her very own eyes. Her baby, the King, is now here, earth side and in her arms.

Mary takes this fresh born babe and ever so tenderly wraps Him in swaddling cloths. The King of kings – Lord of lords – the Great I Am - has just been ever so gently wrapped in cloth by this new, young mother and I have no doubt she held Him close as she brushed her cheek against His, her Savior. Briefly there would have been no thoughts of the hay, the animals, the mix of sweat and manure that hung in the air. Only her and her babe. Everything would seem to stop as they took each other in.

Then, a cow lows bringing them back to reality and the young mother lays her sweet babe in the manger. Her weariness kicks in and she must rest. She must rest while dreamily watching a sleeping Jesus. A moment she will hold close and treasure in her heart for many years.

Sorry to go into so much detail but I can so clearly imagine it all. And ladies, this is what women do. They deal with the circumstances at hand and then lay back wearily and sometimes overwhelmed wondering, now what??

We learn so many things from each season of our lives, not to mention from each tragedy or major event. What we do with all of this, is ultimately what will tell our story of, who and what we are made of, and from Whom we get our strength when we are weak.

It will give us grit and tenacity to share with someone else going through a similar season we are all too familiar with, and help us leave a legacy for our children, grandchildren or those who've known us. For others to know the secret of how, (insert your name in blank) _____ endured, loved, lavished, fought, prayed, survived, knew peace and won the victory to claim freedom in Christ for all eternity. A legacy of Jesus.

So many are stumbling around in adult hood while trying to be productive adults and hoping no one knows what is going on deep inside. All the while trying to rock the whole adult thing when we are just going through the motions. Often this is leaving us as open game for reality to knock us into left field while we are completely unprepared.

Funny, all these "life moments" and we are still expected to show up for work, appointments, meetings, and even Sunday School while looking presentable. Not to mention that husband. Yep, need to be smiling when he comes through the door because who knows what kind of day he had. A woman's life can be exhausting.

Welcome to life, not for the faint of heart part.

We must remember Who created us as we navigate these seasons of life. The evil one likes to keep us off our game enough, just enough to give him a leg up so he can slip and slither in to do further damage. The evil one has a plan, and he's not afraid to use it.

Keeping us off kilter, just enough, is part of the enemy's plan alright. Yep, he has a plan and he's not picky, no one is exempt from trials and turmoil. He loves darkness and that is where he loves to slither in. He came to steal kill and destroy. He is good at what he does. He is, the master manipulator.

While we are being wives, mothers, changing diapers, getting kids ready for school, cooking dinner, headed to our next college class, preparing our Sunday School lesson, career women or just entering a new season of life, and have no idea what to do, etc., the evil one, the master deceiver, is at work.

These my friends are potential battles in the making. Battles - We all get one or some, no one is exempt.

So, how do we prepare for battle? TRUTH! God's Truth is what equips us for God ordained works, both to further His Kingdom and battle the enemy in the realm where spiritual war is far too prevalent!

You see, following Jesus is important, but we are called to do more than mere follow, we are to share Jesus with others. The more we know about Jesus ourselves, the more eager we become to share Him with others. The buck doesn't stop there either.

We should be helping to disciple these new followers of Christ. By discipling these new believers in Jesus, we are helping them build strong foundations of doctrine, creating a perpetual harvest of souls; they love Jesus, they share Jesus, etc., – Kingdom building.

That Truth, His Word, will light our path and bring us closer to Him. Why would we ever want to navigate our way without it?

(Psalm 119:105) Your word is a lamp to my feet and a light to my path.

3
BATTLES

If you had a way of knowing that you were going into battle, what is the one thing that could mean all the difference to you? For me, it would be knowing that I am not alone. Good news, you are not.

I am not talking about the times we blame traffic delays or spilled coffee on satan. No, what I am talking about are direct hits from the evil one. There are times he orchestrates situations in hopes of derailing us or causing life altering events to hold you captive, both mentally and spiritually so you are no longer effective.

When you spill your coffee or stub your toe, you become frustrated, inconvenienced, and may even put you in a bad mood. This is usually not life altering.

However, if the enemy fills you with enough lies that your thoughts are consumed with untruths, you may not be focused on your family, or he could throw you into a deep depression that tries to smother you in darkness. Depression will affect not only you but everyone around you. Then there is always the worst nightmare just lurking...

God forbid if the enemy were to cause the life of someone you dearly love, to be taken too soon. These my friends have the potential to make you ineffective.

The enemy doesn't mind if all day long you call yourself a Christian, as long as you are not an effective one. There are consequences for not being prepared for battle- and this is one of them.

You also need to understand that God doesn't give you these battles. They are usually instigated by the enemy and sometimes, just because we live in a sin filled world. However, God is almighty, and yes, He could stop or avert them. There are times He does just that, and then there are times He will allow the battle. There is a big difference between causing a situation and allowing a situation.

It is also vital to understand that your Lord does NOT leave you alone during these times. You see, in Luke chapter 4, beginning in verse one, this is made clear to us. God's glory is revealed when we persevere during our "desert/wilderness" times. It is during these times we are given the opportunity to shine for Him even if it is through smut covered faces, for those of us who have walked through the fire; through brokenness for those who've been broken or from dry and parched lips for those who've truly longed and desired for more Jesus as the desert beat down on them.

Being in the desert definitely doesn't mean you are alone or abandoned – far from it. Take notice of verse 4 –

(1 of Luke 4), Then Jesus, being filled with the Holy Spirit, ... was led by the Spirit into the wilderness, 2/ being tempted for 40 days by the devil.

This means even in our desert, broken, parched or walked through the fire moments, we are not alone. Where the Spirit leads you, He will see you through – if you will allow it.

Please know, it breaks God's heart to see His children hurting and in pain. God not only knows that He has the power to see you through battles, but also that He can prepare you for those battles; battles that He already knows you will face. When we face these battles prepared, it reminds the enemy Who we belong to, and our Lord gets the glory.

Sometimes life can stink, but God is still on His throne and He is still good. We must lean in to Him NOW and allow Him to help us prepare for the unknown. It can get rough out there, so remember, it's life, and life is not for the faint of heart. He is looking for soldiers on this journey and the Lord knows He designed you to be up for the task.

As believers we should have a Holy Indignation when it comes to our husbands/children, families, knowing the evil one is on the prowl and ready to attack. We need to know we are ready to do battle, a Holy battle. We need to be ready to protect and guide those under our care and those around us - which will in turn, pass down a legacy.

When the enemy attack's he is very strategic in his methods. In other words when he instigates an attack it is not always directly at just us. The "hit" is aimed in such a way that more than one person may very well be affected by this target, or at least crippled by it.

When the enemy's target is for wide effect, he uses the benefit of ripple effects. You see, ripple effects don't just touch you, they touch all those around you. Ripple effects reach out and keep going much like tossing a pebble into a quiet lake. If you notice, the rock causes small ripples that just keep spreading. Ripple effects are powerful when used by the evil one.

This is why, Christian or not, satan will strike, because his aim is to bring down as many at a time as he can.

Oh, and make no mistake, when the enemy's aim is at your spouse, he is most definitely assaulting you too! Your husband is carrying his own burdens. Even if you are mad at your spouse, his attack is yours. The enemy knows this very well.

In chapter 11 (Worth), I mention that we were created to be our spouse's helper, not hinderer. Well, I recommend that you take this seriously. You better fight this battle as if it is yours, because it is.

When your spouse is weak, be strong and vice versa. Afterall, we are to imitate Christ and that is a powerful reflection of Him – "For when I am weak, He is strong." (2 Corinthians 12: 10b)

The more direct attacks are downright spiritual warfare. The small attacks are to wear you down to the point you aren't up for the serious attacks.

This my friends, ladies, sisters on this mission filed, is where satan is banking on you being too busy, too weary, too overwhelmed. He also knows others will be watching you and how you handle everything from the day-to-day issues to the serious crises he sent your way, hoping one of these would bring you crumbling down into a heap. Leaving you feeling worthless to all those around you, still a Christian, but not effective.

If you are weak, weary and overwhelmed, know this – you have not failed! That is only what the enemy wants you to believe, and it is a lie! Remember, he is the father of lies.

(John 8:44) ... There is no truth in him. Whenever he speaks a lie, he speaks from his own nature, for he is

a liar and the father of lies.

Weak, weary and overwhelmed – come to Jesus and tell Him. You do not have to do this alone.

(Matthew 11:28) Come to Me, all who are weary and heavy-laden, and I will give you rest.

If you know my story, then you know I have certainly been battle weary. For those of you who don't, I'll give you a snapshot. Please know I do not share this as a sob story to gain sympathy, oh no! Don't misunderstand me, much of my story is sad, downright heartbreaking – BUT, this is a story of VICTORY and you must hear the sad parts to understand the **MIGHTY VICTORY** my friends.

I have unwanted, firsthand experience with bondage, fear, smothering darkness and soul crushing heartbreak. There is much I will leave out but, I will share with you the worst of the worst so you will better understand where I am coming from. ~ I was blessed with five beautiful children. I had five in nine years and I felt I had the world by the tail – until I didn't.

With five children between the ages of 11 months and 10 years old, well, life was chaotically beautiful if you will. Our afternoons were filled with ball, baton and scouts – evenings were supper, bath and bedtime stories with lots of snuggles. Mornings would often leave us hunting that wayward shoe that would elude us while getting ready for school. Yep, life was chaotic, but good.

One Friday in late October I was picking them up from school. It was a typical ride home. There would be lots of catching up to do about the day. There would be laughter, children talking over one another and occasionally, a disagreement. It was a beautifully typical day.

On our way home we discussed what they would be wearing the next week at school because it would be homecoming week and they had a designated costume day for each school day. We made verbal and mental notes to make sure everyone would have what they needed to kick off the next week.

But you see, life doesn't always go as planned. Nope. When Monday rolled around, I was not helping my little crew get ready for school. Instead, I was picking out three child size caskets.

Sunday afternoon, my 6, 8 and 10-year-old were in a pickup truck headed back to meet us (they had spent the night away). While on their way back home, a drunk driver crossed the center yellow line; hitting, head on, the pickup truck my children were riding in. All three children were killed instantly on impact. My life as I knew it was completely turned upside down and forever changed.

That day I began a journey I did not ask for! You see, sometimes darkness creeps in, slow and easy. Sometimes it comes crashing down on you where you can hardly breath – this time it came crashing out of nowhere, hitting me head on and rocked my world.

I had many instances in my life where reality tried to broadside me. During most of those times, I did not know my Jesus. The difference this time was – I did.

The bad news is - I know intense pain, pain that is humanly impossible to bear. The better than good news is - I also know of a supernatural peace and rest that can be yours in such a time. I wish I could give it to you myself. I cannot. Only He (Jesus) can, and this is why I so eagerly point to Him.

This is why I so urgently beg you to allow God to prepare you for the unknown. The unknown is only unknown until it isn't.

the unknown is only unknown until it isn't

Jesus gives you all you need, but you must be both, willing to let Him do a work within you, and you to be intentional about cultivating your relationship with Him.

You, through Christ, have the chance to take all the ripple effects the enemy intended for darkness, and you my dear, have the opportunity to use them for God's glory. You have the authority to shine light into that darkness and turn the table on the master manipulator himself.

To do this we need to be armed. Once armed, we then can be effective on the battlefield. Once we are armed and on the battlefield, our two greatest advantages in the spiritual realm are:

Standing firm in who we are in Christ & knowing how to weld our Sword (Word of God) ~ This will come from understanding the authority we have because He lives inside of us.

For either of these two things to be effective, we must know who God says He is. Well, He is exactly who He says He is. But, don't take my word for it – take His. If you do not know, that you know, that you know this, then by all means ask HIM to show you who He is. He will. Ask Him and then dig into His Word. Open the Bible and soak up what He has to say to you. Ask Him to reveal what He wants you to know. You will not be disappointed.

God and His Word are one, so when you dig into His Word, it is as though you have crawled right up in His lap for precious time with the very One who created you.

Picture a toddler crawling up in your lap and taking both his hands and placing one on each side of your face and pulling your face close while he talks to you. (Or am I the only one who has had little ones do this to me?)

(John 1:1-5) says, "In the beginning was the Word and the Word was with God and the Word was God. He was in the beginning with God. All things were made through Him and without Him nothing was made that was made. In him was life and the life was the light of men. The light shined into darkness and the darkness did not comprehend it".

That last line - "The light shined into darkness and the darkness did **NOT** comprehend it" That line speaks volumes!

Please hear this- darkness cannot conquer what it cannot comprehend! Darkness can fight you tooth and nail, but it cannot conquer what it does not understand!

If we have accepted Jesus as our Lord and Savior then He is in us. Since He is in us, we then have certain authority, through Him and after all, He can conquer all darkness.

~ We have the authority to come boldly to the throne ~

(Hebrews 4:16) Let us therefore come boldly to the throne of grace, that we may obtain and

find grace to help in time of need.

~We have the authority to make satan flee from us – *(James 4:7) ...Resist the devil and he will flee from you.*

~We have the authority to speak boldly about Jesus and spread the Good News. *(Titus 2:15) Speak these things, exhort, and rebuke with all authority...*

~ We can resist the devil.
> *(Ephesians 6:11) Put on the whole armor of God, that you may be able to stand against the wiles of the devil.*

Speaking of the armor of God...

This is where it is crucial that you understand this is not flesh and blood you are up against – this is spiritual warfare. Don't take my word for it, let's see what the word of God has to say...

> *(Ephesians 6:12) For we do not wrestle against flesh and blood, but against principalities, against powers, against the rulers of the darkness of this age, against spiritual hosts of wickedness in the heavenly places.*

When in warfare that is spiritual, you need something spiritual:

God's Word ~ Salvation ~ Truth ~ Peace ~ Faith
Armor – a covering of protection to protect during
battle.
Now, let's roll that together and see what our Lord
says about putting on the full armor of God.

> *THE ARMOR OF GOD is a vital part*
> *of our being prepared. (Ephesians 6:13-*
> *17) Lays out our armor of God:*
>
> *13/Therefore, take up the full armor of*
> *God, so that you will be able to resist in*
> *the evil day, and having done*
> *everything, to stand firm.*
> *14/ Stand firm therefore, having Gird*
> *your loins with TRUTH, and put on the*
> *BREASTPLATE of RIGHTEOUSNESS*
> *15/ Having SHOD your FEET with the*
> *preparation of the Gospel of Peace*
> *16/ Above all take up the SHEILD OF*
> *FAITH with which you will be able to*
> *extinguish all the flaming arrows of the*
> *evil one.*
> *17/ And take the HELMET of*
> *SALVATION, and the SWORD OF THE*
> *SPIRIT, which is the Word of God.*
> *(Ephesians 6:13-17)*

Seek God Himself and He will give you the
discernment about your authority in Him.

God is not the author of confusion either. So, if you are in a new season of life, nothing bad going on but just aren't sure what comes next or what next looks like- don't let the evil one try and confuse or sidetrack you. God's Word says "For God is not the author of confusion but of peace…" (1Corinthians 14:33)

If you are in Christ, you have complete authority over the evil one.

> *(Romans 8:37) "…We are more than conquerors through Him who loved us."*

You were chosen by the Lord; He will equip you but you must be willing. Do not be afraid and NEVER underestimate the evil one.

Stand firm in who you are in Christ, but first you must understand who you are in Christ. We will dig deeper into this in the chapter on "Worth".

Oh, and make no mistake – this is not a one and done kind of lesson, armor, battle and then you have it all down pat. No, there is cultivation to be done. There is cultivation which will strengthen your foundation with Jesus.

Suit-up ladies ~ it could get rough.

4
SIT & SEEK

BE STILL AND KNOW THAT I AM GOD ~ PSALM 46:10

Make sure you are taking time to "sit & seek". This is crucial, so if you aren't – start. This is the cultivation part of your relationship with Jesus. Growing your relationship and your knowledge and love for the One who loves you like no other.

Sit and seek is exactly what it says it is. It is taking the time to sit, be still and seek the Lord your God with all you've got. I can promise you two things: you won't go wrong and you won't regret it.

Maybe this is something you already do, maybe it is something you used to do and you either let it fall by the wayside or you morphed into just going through the motions and aren't sure what you are really doing anymore.

You see, knowing who God is, is one thing. Experiencing Him is another. Even satan knows who God is. Having and experiencing an intimate relationship with Christ is the beautiful side effect of not just having faith, but exercising that faith.

Having an intimate relationship with Christ is the only thing that fills our emptiness. Experiencing Jesus gives you a firsthand understanding of your worth, and that my friends can be a gamechanger.

When I say an intimate relationship with Jesus Christ, I am not talking about showing up on Sunday's for church. Yes, corporate worship is important for the Christian walk but what I am talking about is different. What I am referring to is so personal that if you don't have your Bible with you, you can still have very special time with your Lord. I love being in His word but one of the beauties of being His and having that incredible relationship is that it can strictly be, just me and Him.

I am talking about spending one-on-one time with Jesus and getting to know Him. Make time to sit and truly seek Him part of your normal routine, as much as picking up your phone is to you first thing each morning.

If you will sit & seek with the Lord, you will find Him, and He will show you unbelievable peace and hope. I do believe one of you just mumbled, "but I don't have time!" To be clear, very clear, I am also not talking about checking off a "quite time" box. Many denominations refer to their time with the Lord as "quiet time". Nothing wrong with labeling your one-on-one time with Him, after all, I evidently call mine, "sit & seek" time.

What I am suggesting, is for you to please not box yourself in for scheduling a quick devotional read just so you can check your box and say, "I'm done for the day".

Nothing wrong with devotionals but this is not where you should try and get your meat from. If you quickly, read through a devotional, just to say "done" - you really haven't accomplished what was intended. Five minutes with the Lord can actually be quite precious – if we have really leaned into Him during that time to soak Him up. It's just NOT about checking off a box folks.

I am also not saying you must spend an hour or two reading the scriptures (that would be awesome but even if time permits, for some of us our ADD would kick in). When you have a personal relationship with Jesus, you can enjoy that with just you and Him. Yes, you need to get in the Bible and soak up His Word but you also need to sit and "soak Him" up. You will appreciate being able to do this the more time you spend with just Him. This is also a good time to not only pour your heart out to Him but to just chat. And very importantly, listen.

My most precious time with Him is usually right after I have been in His Word, soaking up and saturating my mind and soul with His Word. Just sitting and taking it all in.

In this life full of hurry up and let's get busier, we need to heed the scriptures, especially a few that are key to our centering, balance, sanity, core and to our life more abundant. Ladies, we are often led to believe that multitasking is a gift or well-honed skill. Society has even taught us that this will make us a power house and uber successful in today's world. This is not necessarily true.

When I say, heed the scriptures, I am talking about the very Word of God. Not some sweet something someone came up with to make you feel good for the day. Please note, there is nothing wrong with a good devotional. I love to read a good devotional! Devotionals are meant to supplement and compliment your ongoing time in His Word and your relationship with Him, NOT replace it.

However, if that is the only forum you are using to spend time with the Lord and in His Word, you will be sadly disappointed in the long run. Again, if you are looking for fluff, this is not the book for you.

I must caution you as to what you use as a devotional. Make sure it is in line doctrinally with the very Word of God. I have just been amazed at the "good devotionals" that people have wanted to share with me (some were VERY good) but many have been written by someone where the person who wrote them had twisted scripture to make people feel good. I call the ones writing these things or speaking them, "ear ticklers"- the Bible, the Word of God calls them, untaught and unstable people (2 Peter 3:14-18) NKJV.

The Bible actually warns of these people who twist His Word in other places as well.

> *Eph. 5:6 Let no one deceive you with empty words... (2 Cor. 11:13-14) For such men are false apostles, deceitful workers, disguising themselves as apostles of Christ 14/ No wonder, for even satan disguises himself as an angel of light.*

This is why you must spend time in His Word yourself, so you will be able to recognize false doctrine and not be swayed by the world.

Also, it is vital, when you google or search out scripture, in "other" places, to check it against an actual Bible. Don't take the internet's word for it. I have seen where people have tried to just google "God Stuff" only to be led down a path that steered them away from Jesus and into a path that just makes a person feel good for the moment. Folks, that is a temporary feel good, I can promise you that.

When we take up the temporary, we are usually opening the door for other things that are not good.

> *(James 1:14-17) "But each one is tempted when he is drawn away by his own desires and enticed. Then,*

when desire has conceived, it gives
birth to sin; when it is full-grown,
brings forth death. Do not be
deceived, my beloved brethren.
Every good gift and every perfect
gift is from above...

We are such an easily swayed people on our own. This is why it is crucial we don't venture out to try and do life on our own – we need a Holy and perfect God to guide us.

When we dig into His Word we are "leaning in" to Him. When we do this "leaning in" we cannot help but be touched by Him. Let me give you a beautiful example of this from God's Holy Word. This is coming from Luke 7:43-47 where a sinful woman anoints Jesus' Feet. I urge you to read these scriptures yourself. Here is what I see when I close my eyes and imagine these scriptures.

She comes through the door, head down,
*   ashamed to look into the eyes of all*
*   those there. Ashamed to look at those*
*   who know who and what she is.*
* She comes straight to her Master, still*
*   never looking up. She feels the need to*
*   touch Him. She is overwhelmed to be*
*   in His presence – the tears come; they*
*   won't stop.*
She takes His feet now – His feet that are
*   inevitably being washed by her tears.*

His feet are warm in her hands as she tries wiping away her tears with her hair.

She cannot get enough of the love she feels radiating from Him as she kisses His feet- still, she is too ashamed to look up and into His eyes.

She breaks open the oil and pours over these feet that are precious to her – His feet.

She has her hands on His feet and yet she is the one being touched – touched by Him.

As her tears fall, she pours herself out to Him, He absorbs her shame and fills her with love and ultimately with forgiveness.

He takes her chin, lifts her eyes to His and says, "Your sins are forgiven... your faith has saved you, go in peace."

And she is never the same again ~ because this is what happens when we encounter Jesus!

My friends – if you are willing to take time to sit & seek, leaning in to Him – you will be forever changed by Him.

5
SERIOUS BUSINESS

We must get serious because this is serious business. Just turn on the television or pick up a newspaper and you will find yourself slap dab in the middle of serious times. Serious times call for serious measures.

Ladies, this is not the time to just think about or mull over, whether we should get serious. The only question should be, are you willing? The time is now to get serious with our God, with our families, and - serious with our positions on the battlefield! That is exactly what we enter every day when our feet hit the floor.

This is serious stuff. There are a few things you will need if you want to be serious about navigating the "now what" in your life and surviving the things this world throws at us along the way.

God has called women for mighty things earth side. You need to understand that God doesn't call us last minute to do something. He has called us from the start and the "along the way" part is where He prepares us. We have been both known and called from the womb.

> *(Galatians 1:15) But when God, who had set me apart even from my mother's womb and called me through His grace... / (Jeremiah 1:5) Before I formed you in the womb, I knew you, and before you were born I consecrated you..."*

There are times we may not understand our calling or what our purpose is – but He does. He is also using this time to prepare us for that calling and purpose.

If we are to be well prepared for what He has called us to, we need to be intentional and diligent about our relationship with Him. We must also take seriously our time to rest. We must rest to refresh our soul. The best rest is when we rest in Jesus.

> *(Matt 11:28 &29) Come to Me, all you who are weary and are heavy laden, and I will give you rest. 29/...and you will find rest for your souls.*

You see, satan loves our modern society and all that we have bought into. The busier and more chaotic we allow our lives to be, the more he is likely to get a foot hold into our lives. This is why our intentionality and diligence towards our relationship with Jesus is so vital.

Women were a big part of Christ's ministry. If you will look at Luke 8: 1-3 you will see that Jesus had women who traveled with Him and His disciples to learn from Him and to fellowship with Him. You see, these women, these followers of Jesus, were eager and readily willing to follow Him because they had been touched by Him. When we have been touched by Jesus and share this with others, we are planting seeds for Him and His Kingdom. This can ultimately lead others to experiencing Jesus too.

Another important nugget is for us to allow God to cut the sin out of our lives so we may feel His presence. This doesn't mean that all of a sudden, we never face temptation or ever have a bad thought again. Even Jesus was tempted. In (Matthew 4:1) Then Jesus was led up by the Spirit into the wilderness to be tempted by the devil. (Luke 4:2) Jesus was tempted for 40 days by the devil. Being tempted is not a sin, it's what we do with that temptation that can either lead to sin or remind the enemy Who we belong to.

Sin in our lives hinders our fellowship with our heavenly Father and why would we ever want to do that when we need Him so much.

(Galatians 5:7) ...Who hindered you from obeying the truth?

(2 Corinthians 7:10) For Godly sorrow produces repentance leading to salvation, not to be regretted; but the sorrow of the world produces death.

(James 5:16b) The effective, fervent prayer of a righteous man avails much.

(Colossians 3:2) Set your mind on things above, not on things on the earth.

(Philippians 4:8) Finally brethren, whatever is true, whatever is honorable, whatever is pure, whatever is lovely, whatever is of good repute, if there is any excellence and if anything, worthy of praise. Dwell on these things.

This means that we should be intentional about our focus and where that focus really lays. We can't hide our sin from God, no matter how hard we try. If you dig into Joshua chapters 7 & 8 you will see what I am talking about here. The good news is that if you allow the Lord to cut the sin out of your life you not only will be able to feel His presence but you will also be able to stand before your enemies.

Wow, I don't know about you but in this world

full of troubles and chaos, I sure could use some
confidence for all that I will be able to face and
withstand.

Many of us are so busy just trying to survive the
day, all while smiling. Sometimes we smile because
we don't dare want the world to know what lies
beneath our smiles and nods.

We may not want the world to know, but Jesus
knows. He knows and He is there for you.

It's important that we take scripture seriously.
God and His Word are one (just look back at John 1:1)
We are to not just read/hear scripture. We are to
HEED it -EARNESTLY HEED it. We are to be
diligent, down right intentional with the Word of God.
Or we will drift away.

(Hebrews 2:1) Therefore we
must give the more earnest
heed to the things we have
heard, lest we drift away.

It is telling us to hang on to the Truth so we
don't drift. As my friend Gwynn says, "We are not here
to avoid the world; we are here to engage". Our God
has equipped us, not just to be-bop idly through this
life, but for Kingdom works. It is His truth which
ultimately equips us for such.

This is why it is so vital that we don't just hear
the Truth but KNOW THE TRUTH. Soak it up and

soak it in. Saturate yourself in His Word.

Drifting, this is what boats do when not firmly in place or on course - just drifting. When you are intentional and diligent about God's Word, you my friend, become firmly rooted. When rooted, you don't drift.

> *(Colossians 2:6&7) As you therefore received Christ Jesus the Lord, so walk in Him, rooted and built up in Him and established in the faith...*

We don't want to just represent Him. We want to represent Him well. Remember, we want to leave a Jesus legacy.

~Let's recap those few things we need to "get serious"

1 – Cut out Sin (Confess your sin to Jesus)
2 – Rest
3 – Heed the Holy Scriptures
4 – Don't Drift

Let me guess, you still think you are too busy. Let me share a little about someone I admire, yet I have never met. Also, she had to be the busiest person on the planet. I cannot read her story without weeping for the, hero for the Kingdom, I feel she was. Her ripple effects are still being felt today.

Susanna Wesley (born 1669 – died 1742).

Susanna was known for being the mother of Charles and John Wesley. These two brothers helped found the Methodist Church as you know it today.

John Wesley, one of her sons, was an English Theologian who was a leader in a major revival within the Church of England. But let's back up. These two brothers were not her only children. Susanna birthed 19 children with 10 surviving. She homeschooled all of the children, cooked for them, ran their home, and much more. (note- there were no modern conveniences)

Her husband was often gone so basically, everything fell to her. Her life was not easy. (You should read her whole story)

As I shared earlier, I myself had 5 children in nine years. I know what my household was like during the day. I cannot even begin to fathom what a household with 10 children would be like. How was she able to handle such a task you may ask? JESUS.

She spent much time in the Word. One of you just blinked about five times thinking, "How did she do that?!". During the day she would take the time to sit down, with her Bible in her hand. She would then pull her apron over her head and spend time with Him and in His Word. I have no doubt that the children learned pretty quickly not to mess with mama when her apron was over her head.

Susanna, a woman who was diligent in being about her Father's business. There in the tent of her apron, she and the Lord did business. She prayed, she read, she wept and she no doubt leaned in to the One who could give her rest. She raised and trained her children in the Lord. She was serious about her God and her family. Therefore, leaving a mighty powerful legacy.

I say all that to say this – if you are serious about your relationship with your Jesus, then be intentional and diligent.

Actually, I would say that Susanna began each day with "premeditated purpose" and we should do the same.

Just what could it mean for us, our homes and the Kingdom, if we began each day with ~ Premeditated Purpose and solid erudition (using God's Word to glean this erudition)? I believe the outcome would place us in a Radically Intentional mode with our Jesus. In other words -we would be on fire.

6
PRAYING

Praying is one of the sweetest experiences you can have with your Jesus and is not to be taken lightly. Do not underestimate the power of prayer. This thing called prayer is not only sweet but, is ultimately one of your greatest weapons when it comes to spiritual warfare. This is a weapon that can downright demolish strongholds.

> *(2 Corinthians 10:3-4) For though we walk in the flesh, we do not war according to the flesh. 4/ For the weapons of our warfare are not carnal but mighty in God for pulling down strongholds.*

Again, do not underestimate the power of prayer.

Praying doesn't have to be eloquent and long. Frankly it doesn't even really have to make sense to us. Have you ever been so upset you could barely talk? If we are in Christ then we have the Holy Spirit in us to interpret our prayers to the Father.

(Romans 8:26) "...the Spirit also helps in our weaknesses. For we do not know what we should pray for as we ought, but the Spirit Himself makes intercession for us with groanings which cannot be uttered".

Right there, just chat, pour your heart out or sit and weep until you can weep no more. Our Father in heaven hears. He even catches our tears, now that's love! (Psalm 56:8) *...You put my tears in a bottle...*

Praying is talking with our Lord. It's communing with Him. It's spending intimate time letting down walls, and letting God do what God does. So, let me ask you – do you have enough conversations with your Lord to know His voice?

The more time spent with Him, the more we will know His voice.

Our Lord wants to share so many things with us, but He wants us to ask. By our asking it shows an intentional act on our part. In His Word, He actually tells us, *"Call to Me, and I will answer you, and show*

you great and mighty things, which you do not know."
(Jeremiah 33:3)

Your church building and your physical Bible can be stripped away from you but, no one can stop you from praying. You can pray with your eyes open or closed, while speaking out loud or in your head and heart.

While praying with other believers is incredible and important *(Matt. 18:20) For where two or three are gathered together in My name, I am there in the midst of them.* When multiple believers come together in His name to lift up prayers, mighty things can happen.

However, it is also very important to find regular time to pray while alone. This was something that even Jesus did. He would get away from the crowd and pray, spending time with His Father in heaven.

> *(Mark 1:35) Now in the morning, having risen long before daylight, He went out and departed to a solitary place; and there He prayed.*

There are other scriptures that speak of this as well: Luke 5:15-16, Luke 6: 12-13 and Matt. 14:23. Finding time alone with our heavenly Father renews us, allows our soul to take a deep breath and gives us strength to face the day.

Being obedient means praying regularly. We are not to worry about an outcome – our job is to obey.

> *(Ephesians 6:18-20) Praying always with all prayer and supplication in the Spirit, being watchful to this end with all perseverance and supplication for all the saints 19/ and for me, that utterance may be given to me, that I may open my mouth boldly to make known the mystery of the gospel; 20/ for which I am an ambassador in chains; that in it I may speak boldly, as I ought to speak.*

Pray and He will give you the discernment of when to be bold. We are to be anxious for nothing and to give much thanks.

> *(Philippians 4:6) Be anxious for nothing, but in everything by prayer and supplication, with thanksgiving, let your requests be made known to God 7/ and the peace of God, which surpasses all understanding, will guard your hearts and minds through Christ Jesus.*

(James 5:13) Is anyone among you suffering? Let him pray. Is anyone cheerful? Let him sing psalms.

Singing is a precious way to spend time with your Lord. Time with Him is special and does not need to be structured.

(1 Thessalonians 5:16-18) Rejoice always, 17/ pray without ceasing, 18/ in everything give thanks; for this is the will of God in Christ Jesus for you.

Praying for God's will to be done and not ours is sometimes difficult, but this is effective praying ladies. This is part of our surrender – His will, not ours.

Praying is a form of worship as well. Take Psalm 103 for example. The whole chapter is pure worship. Whether you read it aloud, sing it loud and proud or soft and sweet. This chapter alone is worthy of bringing out a box of tissues if you pay attention to the words and no doubt, brings God glory and honor.

Make prayer a habit and it will become second nature, just like breathing is. You will feel His presence like never before.

7
WHISPERS OF THE ENEMY

The enemy is quite clever and cunning. He is not always brazened or bold. Many times, he just whispers and is extremely persistent. You need to be more persistent, do not become complacent about replacing the enemy's lies with God's Truth.

Being that the evil one is clever, he uses repetition. The point of this repetition of course is to permeate our psyche, mind games if you will. Too many of us become familiar with these whispers. The master deceiver is quite methodical with this technique.

Often the whispers come more frequently at night. You need to rest and it's dark, the enemy is waiting, waiting to divert your sleep and thoughts.

The whispers make you feel heavy. Your mind and body have been targeted. You now feel heavy, tired and just plain weighed down. In spite of being tired, you may not sleep well either.

In the Word of God, we have been warned to be very aware, and we should heed that warning.

(1 Peter 5:8) Be sober, be vigilant; because your adversary the devil walks about like a roaring lion, seeking whom he may devour.

That adversary is well aware of both, our insecurities and the major and exhausting loads we carry as women. So, he whispers and lets that seep deep, into our psyche.

The evil one plays these mind games to cause you to…

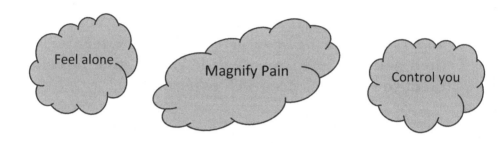

(Much could be added here - but you get the idea)

Bottom line – It's to make you ineffective for the Kingdom!

Whispers of the enemy are powerful, **DO NOT UNDERESTIMATE** him!

The whispers of the enemy **ARE LIES! DO NOT BUY THE LIES!**

Replace those lies with the Truth – with God's **TRUTH.** When you spend time in God's Word soaking up His Truth: FIRST – it is harder to accept the enemy's lie. Two – use the scripture and speak it out loud. (In the chapter on Worth I cover this more)

Many times, satan will just befuddle us so much that we are tempted to return to what is familiar, even when that means unhealthy or abusive situations. In other words, we may return to bondage of our own accord. That's a pretty scary thought but it happens all the time. Hang in there and I promise that the healthy can become your familiar.

A common antic I see used by the evil one is to make us feel unclean, and unforgiven. Have you ever noticed how much easier it is for us to forgive others than it is for us to forgive ourselves? The enemy sure knows about this and he uses it to his advantage. Even satan knows that we have been forgiven of our sins.

The enemy can't change that, but, what if he could constantly remind us of the ugliness in our pasts? Yep – he has struck a gold mine when we let him use this one. Don't let the master manipulator get away with this!

If the very God who created you can forgive you – then my dear, you need to accept it, as unworthy as any of us are, there is a reason you were forgiven and your Jesus needs you to carry on as a forgiven child of His. Don't let the enemy or any man tell you otherwise.

These next few scriptures tell it like it is. That we have been wiped clean and forgiven, period. We must really accept what our Jesus has done for us.

(Colossians 2: 11-15) "In Him you were also circumcised with the circumcision made without hands, by putting off the body of the sins of

flesh, by the circumcision of Christ, 12/ buried with Him in baptism, in which you also were raised with Him through faith in the working of God, who raised Him from the dead. 13/ And you, being dead in your trespasses and the uncircumcision of your flesh, He has made alive together with Him, having forgiven you all trespasses, 14/ having wiped out the handwriting of requirements that was against us, which was contrary to us. And He has taken it out of the way, having nailed it to the cross. 15/ Having disarmed principalities and powers, He made a public spectacle of them, triumphing over them in it." (Colossians 2: 11-15)

This is one of many reasons it is vital to seek the Lord with **ALL YOUR HEART,** not haphazardly.

(Jeremiah 29:12-14a) "Then you will call upon Me and go and pray to Me, and I will listen to you 13/ And you will seek Me and you will find Me, when you search for Me with ALL YOUR HEART. 14/ I will be found by you, says the Lord, and I will bring you back from your

captivity..."

When we are focused on Jesus, we are not as easily swayed. Therefore, I cannot stress enough how important it is to **TRULY** seek Him and what this will mean in your overall life. So often we use excuses to sin just so we can mentally justify what we are doing. The evil one sees right through this, and by the way, so does God.

The enemy is fully aware that when you purposefully sin, you are allowing yourself to be enslaved. The enemy would love nothing more than to wear you down so you will give in. The evil one knows where we are vulnerable and what our weaknesses are - and he will use them.

Let's take a close look at what God's word says about the enemy and his position.

> *(John 10:10) The thief does not come except to steal, and to kill and to destroy. I have come that they may have life and that they may have it more abundantly.*

I hope you caught the part about "life more abundant"! Jesus is serious about this.

Notice that the scripture reads "does not come except to" in referring to the enemy. That reference is from the **NKJV**. In the **NASB** uses the phrase, "comes only to". The **KJV** (and you have to love this) says, "cometh not but to". Either way, the enemy's mission is the same, he is out to make you ineffective for the Kingdom.

You see, he can make you ineffective but he cannot remove your salvation. You need to fully understand this. Once you belong to Jesus, **NOTHING, NO ONE**, can pluck you from His hand. Jesus Himself tells us this!

> *(John 10:28) And I give them eternal life, and they shall never perish; neither shall anyone snatch them out of My hand. Your salvation is secure.*

Now we need to make sure our effectiveness remains secure for the Kingdom.

This is a critical time to remember Who you belong to! Call on the name of your Jesus and repeat often. There is power in the very utterance of His name. Be bold about calling on Jesus.

This is a very good reason to memorize scripture. I know, I know. So often I hear people say memorizing scripture is too hard. Should we talk about the words to songs you can recite? Ha-ha, I really do understand. Do you know why you can recall the songs but not the scriptures? You repeat the songs but not the scripture. Funny that we don't think twice about singing a song over and over and yet we aren't as willing to repeat scripture.

Writing the scripture out is key as well in memorizing. Write, recite, repeat. That is the key. Repetition, repetition, repetition. You will not regret memorizing scripture and let me tell you reason number one – when we are able to recall scripture it unleashes the power of God. Take that satan.

8
SHALOM

Shalom is the familiar Hebrew word for Peace.

Personally, I've had enough turmoil in my life that I treasure peace. Peace allows us to stand firm, remain stable and keep a sane mind during the storms, AKA, battles. Peace gives us an inner calmness that can come from no other place, but Jesus.

I spent too many of my years being afraid and living in fear- of both the known and the unknown. Freedom from that fear is amazing and no one should live in fear. It is actually a choice. So, choose wisely.

If you haven't felt that peace from your Jesus lately, I encourage you to get with Him and talk to Him about it. He wants to freely give this as a gift and blessing to us, but we also have free will. When we reject Him, we reject His gifts and blessings.

It has to be our choice to accept this peace the same way it is our choice if we choose Jesus. We must intentionally choose a personal relationship with Him. Flippantly saying we are Christian or just showing up on Sunday to church does not make us a Christian. Same way getting Baptized does not make us a believer either.

Baptism is an outward, public and very beautiful, symbol of our belonging to Christ and that the "old" has been washed away and we have been made new in Christ. I think baptism is a beautiful thing to do and I believe all believers should do this if it is available to them, but, the act itself is not what gives us eternal life. Only Jesus can do that.

Spending time with Jesus is necessary to cultivate your relationship. You are still saved if you accept Jesus as your Lord and Savior even if within seconds you die. Yes, you will enter Heaven for all eternity.

But, but, but – if you have more time than mere seconds, why would you not want to get to know The One who loves you like no other. The One who can see you through anything that otherwise would be humanly impossible to bear. The One who can fill you with such peace that it seems incomprehensible, because it's supernatural. Frankly, once I experienced His peace, there was NO way I would ever want to live without it.

Peace is a gift from Him.

> *(John 14:27) Peace I leave with you, My peace I give to you; not as the world gives do I give to you. Let not your heart be troubled, neither let it be afraid.*

Peace is a blessing.

> *(Psalm 29:11) The Lord will give strength to His people; The Lord will bless His people with peace.*

Seek Him and seek His peace.

> *(Psalm 34:14b) ... Seek peace and pursue it.*

Spend that intimate time with Him, He wants to lavish, love and shower you with so much.

The very God who does not need you – He wanted you, all of you, and He wants you now.

As you dig deeper into your relationship with Jesus, the closer you become with Him, the more He will "multiply" your peace.

> *(2 Peter 1:2) "Grace and peace be multiplied to you in the knowledge of God and of Jesus our Lord, ... through the knowledge of Him who called us by glory and virtue, by which have been given to us exceedingly great and precious promises..."*

I myself will be happy to take exceedingly great and precious promises! I am not sure why anyone would not.

At the end of the day, the Lord is the only One who loves us unconditionally, the only One who will fight for us and Who can give us that peace that passes all understanding. (Eph 2:14) tells us *"For He Himself is our peace"*. Jesus is our peace... He came to not just give us life but life more abundantly and that my friends means, peace.

So why don't we take Him up on that? Jesus is willing to lavish us with love and give us gifts and blessings of peace, amazing. I don't know about you, but peace is priceless to me.

In Luke 8:48 Jesus tells us to "...Go in peace." It is important to understand that peace doesn't always mean quietly.

We are to spread the good news. If we have been touched by Jesus why would we not want to share? Especially if planting that seed could lead others to experiencing Him as well.

9

BE BOLD

Boldness   ~   willingness to take risks and act innovatively; confidence or courage. Not to be confused with brazen, belligerent, arrogant or disrespectful. This boldness, comes from the Lord (Acts 4:13-31).

A boldness that comes only from Christ is a boldness that others may wonder over. There is a time to be bold, and a time not to be. When we belong to Christ, and are in regular communication with Him, we will know when to be bold and how to use boldness that will glorify Him.

As His, we are allowed to come boldly before the throne.

(Hebrews 4:16) Let us therefore come boldly to the throne of grace, that we

may obtain mercy and find grace to
help in time of need.

He doesn't just tell us to come boldly, but to do so without fear. There are just some days I need to park myself right there at the foot of the throne of grace, and not move, just soak it all up! Speaking for myself, there are just "those" days where I need me a whole lot more grace and mercy. Who would really want to turn down a good dose of Grace?! "Not I" says me, the one who knows how weak she is (that is me with a capitol M.E. (I'm hoping somebody threw an amen in there with me.)

In (Ephesians 3:12) Paul tells us (that through Jesus Christ) We have boldness and access with confidence through faith in Him.

(Prov 28:1) The wicked flee when
no one pursues, BUT the righteous
are bold as a lion.

I can tell you right now that ANY boldness I have ever had, much less utilized, most definitely came from the Lord. I don't have a bold bone in my body. As I have grown older, I have gotten bolder about sharing my Jesus and with standing on what is right when circumstances call for me to "stand" on an issue. I can honestly tell you that is only because through time, precious time with Him, He has given me that boldness. I also have learned that I answer to God not man. (That alone gives me more gumption in my boldness)

There will be a time, probably more than once, especially as the times we are currently living in seem to be drawing to a much more wicked end, that you my dear, will need some boldness. And I am talking about a supernatural boldness that man can't explain.

Spend time with Him, seek Him and ask for boldness – it will be given along with (vs 33) Grace and (34) you will lack nothing.

(Acts 5: 29) ... We ought to obey God rather than men.

This my friends will take boldness at times.
Boldness is not to be misused.

So why do we let ourselves get so caught up in trying to please men? Many of us are people pleasers by nature, even when stating that we are not. People may not let it show outwardly but inside, deep inside, they are eager to please and receive affirmation from others.

We are bombarded by magazines, media and our family, friends and neighbors, all so eager to show us how we need to eat, dress, drive, live and so on. (and heaven help that brand new mama who is getting more "how to do's" with that new baby than she can shake a stick at!)

It's so easy to find ourselves feeling different or as though we don't fit in. Feeling like you don't fit in is not just a middle school problem. So why do we struggle so to want to fit in? Again, many are people pleasers.

We should embrace our differences. God did not create us to be just like everyone else.

As a matter of fact, in His Word we are told, *"do not be conformed to this world, BUT be transformed by the renewing of your mind, that you may prove what is that good and acceptable and perfect will of God". (Romans 12:2)*

Whether it be consciously or subconsciously, we often find ourselves thinking we are not up to certain tasks. We think we are not good enough or that we should be a little smarter. Education is very important but I can tell you right now that if God called you to it, He most definitely has or will equip you. Your job is to be willing, no excuses.

This morning I was reading in Luke chapter 1. In this chapter the angel Gabriel has come before Zacharias to say he and Elizabeth will have a son. The angel even goes on to tell Zacharias how great the son will be and that he, the son, will prepare the way for the Lord. Do you know what ol' Zach's reaction is? Basically, he looks at the angel and says, "But we old?!" (I am paraphrasing!) That is the jest of it. He is throwing out an excuse. Forget the fact that an angel of the Lord has appeared to give him this amazing news. He's full of an excuse as to why this can't happen (we old).

Due to old Zach's "unbelief" he was made mute until the child was born. Oh my goodness, if the Lord made us mute today every time we weren't believing – we would be a mighty quiet bunch!

Don't ever think you are too old for the good Lord to use you!! As a matter of fact, if you zip on down in (Luke 1:37) it reads, *"For with God nothing will be impossible"*.

Don't underestimate our Lord. When we are full of excuses what we are really saying is, "I don't believe you God."

When we are not bold, we are not courageous. The enemy loves this.

Be bold in your believing God, be bold for what is right, be bold for your family, be bold for Jesus. Because, boldness is required at times while building your legacy.

If you will remember, back in the chapter on "Seasons", we talked about leaving a legacy, a Jesus Legacy.

The path you are now on in your journey, has you building this legacy. Because it my dear, is part of your purpose and calling. Yes, your legacy is part of your calling and purpose. This is a mighty powerful gift to pass on and leave to future generations. This will live on longer than you or I will walk this earth.

10
PURPOSE

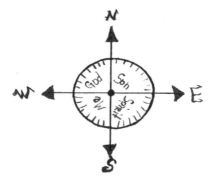

While on this journey we call life, we are either on a path headed toward our purpose or we are already living it out. Along the way, there may be detours. These detours can stop us in our tracks or show us we can bulldoze through. Folks, this is called life, life with battles.

Often, we tend to think that battles only come at certain times but I have learned, the hard way, that there is no rhyme or reason. I take that back, there is a reason, and it is the enemy doing what the enemy does.

We must be battle ready. There is a time for us to pick up the sword and there is a time to allow our Lord to do the fighting for us.

You may be thinking, "I just want to know what my purpose is, I am not looking for a battle." The thing is, if you belong to Jesus, you get both. If you know what your purpose is – fabulous, keep reading and we will get past the "how to find your purpose". You see, often our purpose seems multifaceted.

If you do not know what your purpose is, ask God to show you. Most importantly, be still and listen. You can ask God for something til' the cows come home, but, if you haven't stopped to really listen, you won't hear Him.

This is where we need to know if we are asking God to show us His purpose or -are we asking Him to bless a plan/purpose we think we want? There is a difference.

Let me give you an example of the relevance of paying close attention when He speaks/calls us to do something. One of the ladies I interviewed is now 82 years old. Years ago, she and some other ladies had been traveling to a nearby town for a group ladies Bible study. One day as they were leaving, she felt her heart "prick" about these Bible studies. She shared with me that she felt the Lord impressing on her that they (the ladies) could do this right at their own church/area.

So, that is exactly what she did. She shared the idea and began holding local Bible studies at our church. What began as a group of about eight ladies has now morphed into around 80 ladies getting together and digging into God's Word to study and learn more about their Savior. (this number is pre-covid)

This one lady knew how precious her own Bible study and time with the Lord was. Her love of her Jesus naturally guided her to disciple other women which in turn led them to dig into the Word of God and strengthened their own walk with Jesus.

Folks, she planted seeds for future Kingdom workers and the harvest is still coming in. Talk about ripple effects! One of the blessings that is most dear to her heart today, is that both her daughters are now teachers with the current Bible studies.

I will interject here that one of our callings as women, is for us to be an example to the younger women. (check out Titus 2:3-5) I had some amazing, godly role models when I both, came to know my Jesus and thereafter.

For this I will always be extremely thankful. This means we need to always be aware that others (especially the younger ones) are watching us. This doesn't mean we have to be perfect – it means we are willing to own up when we are not.

In Luke 5 Jesus asked some fishermen to leave all of their possessions and to follow Him. Good news, you do not have to leave your possessions to be souled out, or fully devoted to Jesus. Now, if you feel called to sell or give away all of your possessions and become a missionary – then go for it. Not everyone is called to do that. Praise God for the ones who are and do but, this is for the rest of us. Let Jesus be your obsession and passion, and your purpose will fall into place.

Sure, you can pay attention to things like, what is something that gets you excited and that you seem to just have a natural gift or love of (ask friends, bet they can tell you that much). But you must be willing to accept that even if you are ready to dive into "your purpose", that the timing may not be in line with God's timing. This doesn't always make sense to us. Meanwhile, keep putting one foot in front of the other, even if slowly, keep moving until the time is right. We don't always have to understand, we just have to trust God.

(Isaiah 55:8-9) "For My
thoughts are not your
thoughts, nor are your ways
My ways," says the Lord. 9/
"For as the heavens are
higher than the earth, so are
My ways higher than your
ways, and My thoughts
than your thoughts."

Make sure you are talking with your Jesus about your purpose. Seek Him and talk with the Lord about it, you will get it figured out when the time is right. You must stop and listen or all the asking won't matter. Also be willing to say, "Okay Lord, here I am". Know that if He calls you, He will equip you. Also know that it could be a rocky path.

The Lord is ever aware that our path is not always easy, but our God will go before us. We must trust. When led from bondage the Israelites were not led through the nearest route.

(Exodus 13:17) ...for God
said, "Lest perhaps the
people change their minds
when they see war, and
return to Egypt.".

He knows our nature and so often we would rather go back to the comfy and familiar bondage if things seem to be uncomfortable or hard. We often don't like hard. We need to trust and persevere. When things get tough, we need to look to our Lord.

It is in Chapter 14 of Exodus when we hear "Don't be afraid and see what the Lord will do. My favorite of those verses is in vs. 25 of that chapter and the Egyptians are steadily after the Israelites and God is really not making it easy for them - the Egyptians end up saying, (Ex. 14:25) … "Let us flee from the face of Israel, for the Lord fights for them…".

I read somewhere, that what doesn't kill you - knows Who you belong to. The passage in Exodus makes me think of that. Ladies, when we are living in such a way that the enemy knows Who fights for us – that is a battle we should not fear. Keep in mind that not liking something and not fearing it are two different things.

We often feel as though we should have our act together before we follow Jesus or even before we come to Him in time of need. We don't have to be perfect to follow Him because when we allow Him into our lives, He will slowly mold us into His image (we will not be completely perfected until we see Him face to face).

(Philippians 1:6) …He who began a good work in you

*will perfect it until the day
of Christ Jesus.*

Also, and praise God for this, Jesus doesn't wait for us to get our act together so He can use us either.

Just ask these long-ago women of the Bible:

Sarah – She was old and tired of waiting. She took matters into her own hands because she had trouble believing Gods promises to her. She blamed others when things went wrong. Yet, God used her.

Rahab – She was a prostitute. Yet, God used her.

Martha – She was overly concerned with details and tended to feel sorry for herself. Yet, she believed in Jesus.

Mary Magdalene – Jesus had to drive seven demons out of her. Yet she was a faithful follower of Jesus.

This list could go on and on.

God is not looking for someone who can tidy up their lives really fast and say, "Okay, now, I am ready." Oh no, what He wants is for you to say, "Here I am, just as I am".

Mary, the mother of Jesus is a great example of this! When the angel came to her to let her in on the fact that she would carry within her very own womb and birth our Lord and Savior, she didn't throw out excuses.

(Luke 1:38) "Behold, the maidservant of the Lord! Let it be to me according to your word."

Folks, this was her, "here I am -just as I am" moment. She was probably wondering many things, but she did not hesitate to say, here I am.

The Gospel is a "Just as I am" Gospel ~ not a let me get my act together first, Gospel. Frankly, I am grateful for that. Grace is an incredible thing. God is looking for a willing and humble heart. He is looking for you.

Because you belong to Him, even with your imperfections, He will still fight for you, and what a beautiful thing for the enemy to know Who fights for you.

(Exodus 14:25 - so live in such a way that the enemy knows the Lord fights for you)

(James 1:2-3) ...Count it all joy when you fall into various

trials, knowing that testing of your faith produces patience.

Also, (Romans 5:3) And not only that, but we also glory in tribulations, knowing that tribulation produces perseverance; and perseverance, character; and character, hope.

I don't know about y'all but boy do I need some perseverance, character and hope. He is building our character for the Kingdom work that lay ahead of us and hope, well, hope is why I am able to get out of bed every day. My hope is in Jesus.

HOPE, HOPE, HOPE!!!! Yes, give me Jesus and give me HOPE. They go together like shrimp and grits, chicken and dumplings, cobbler and ice-cream. Seriously, you can't have one without the other- or who would want to. Jesus IS my hope.

A very vital part of this is where wisdom comes in. I am not talking about fancy degrees and higher education. I am talking about a wisdom and knowledge that comes from One place and One place only. Jesus. Do not hesitate, just ask.

In this big ol' world full of "worldly"

people or Christians who the enemy uses on a regular basis, yep, the enemy loves to use born again believers. Many people, just because they do not know Jesus, will not have your best interest at heart. God's got your back in those times as well!

> *(Genesis 50:20) But as for you, you meant evil against me; but God meant it for good...*

It is true that what the world means for harm The Almighty Himself can turn it into something that is good. You may be more familiar with this scripture in Romans –

> *(Romans 8:28) And we know that all things work together for good to those who love God, to those who are the called according to His purpose.*

This does not mean that you like what you are going through at the moment. It does mean to trust, hang in there and God will make things right. You will be blessed, have hope.

Earlier I mentioned that I cling to hope and that it is hope that keeps me hanging in there. For better clarification, it is Jesus whom

I cling to (again my hope is in Him). I believe I mention this in my first book, *From a Mother's Heart a Story of Tragedy and Hope.* I talk about clinging to Jesus like a mad woman. There is a verse in Deuteronomy that I love and almost burst into tears with joy the first time I read it.

> *(Deut. 30:20) That you may love the Lord your God, that you may obey His voice, and that you may* cling to Him, for He is your life and the length of your days...

Ladies, I am telling you – you need to be clinging to Jesus like your life depends on it – because it does! Your sanity and your life depend on Jesus.

> *(James 1:5) If any of you lacks wisdom, let him ask of God, who gives to all liberally and without reproach, and it will be given to him.6/ but let him ask in faith, with no doubting for he who doubts is like a wave of the sea driven and tossed by the wind.*

Good news though – if you are spending that one-on-one time with Jesus, wisdom and understanding are some of the beautiful by-products that come from a deeply intimate relationship with the Great I AM.

If we just use some of that "nevertheless I will" mindset that Simon had in Luke 5, oh the blessings we will reap. In verse 4 Jesus had said to Simon, *"Launch out into the deep and let down your nets for a catch."* Now this had come after a night of fishing with nothing to show for it.

(Luke 5:5) "Master, we have toiled all night and caught nothing; nevertheless, at Your Word I will let down the net."

By doing so, Simon was blessed by his nets being so full that they broke.

May we have a "Just as I am" and a "nevertheless I will", all for Jesus and may our nets be full to breaking with His abundant blessings when we truly surrender.

Our Lord already knew, you would face much in this world – but, you were His creation and He would not just throw you to the world. That choice would be up to you.

*(Jeremiah 29:11) For I
know the thoughts I have
for you, says the Lord,
thoughts of peace and not
of evil, to give you a
future and hope.*

He already knows what He has in store for us, our job is to be intentional, diligent, focused on Him and obey – trust Him and He will guide you with your purpose.

You see, we can search all lifelong for our purpose, but it will be a moot point if in all of our searching we never sought Him.

(Psalm 37:4) Delight yourself also in the Lord, and He shall give you the desires of your heart.

11

WORTH

Consider how precious a soul must be when both God and the devil are after it ~ Charles Spurgeon

Jesus didn't treat women as inferior—so why do we buy into the "not good enough" and inferiority complexes? You are not mediocre. You are special and have been set apart and called to a higher calling by your Lord and savior.

Jesus fully understood how vital women were. The hand that rocks the cradle is a mighty powerful thing. The woman that is a true helper to her husband (not a hinderer).

God designed us that way, the helper part not hinder part. The Lord even says that it is not good for man to be alone, so He created us and then says, it is good. I believe that is pretty powerful.

> *(Genesis 2:18) "And the Lord God said," It is not good that man should be alone; I will make him a helper comparable to him."*

We are each so very uniquely made. He gave us each different gifts and talents and we should use them wisely.

I believe He designed us to be a force to be reckoned with, (where the enemy is concerned, whether we know it or not yet) for several reasons.

One – He created us, He is the Master of creating Masterpieces, SO, you my dear are a beautiful masterpiece.

Two- He made you soft and beautiful, caring and nurturing.

Three- yet, He made you firm and strong from the inside out. Delicate enough to be comforting and caring and strong enough to bear children. Heaven help anyone who tries to harm one of our young.

Four- He gave us strong and sharp minds. We manage a household while planning activities for multiple children, help with homework, give medical attention, plan meals, cook said meals, all while juggling the kids and thinking about all there is still to do before she lays head on her pillow.

Running a home properly takes a business mind. This is whether you work outside your home or not, much and most, it seems, still fall to the lady of the home. You may never have thought about that, or you may know this all too well. It just seems to be the way it is.

It takes strategic time management and just enough structure to keep things running smoothly with rhyme and reason while still allowing for the people in said household to feel loved, cared for and valued.

We must be very careful though; in this big old world we can get so busy managing everything else we forget to take care of ourselves. DON'T. Remember, your rest is critical. We were fearfully and wonderfully made (Psalm 139:14) that scripture also says we should praise Him for that and that His works are marvelous. We are marvelous works of His creations ~ wow! Let that sink in.

Yes, rest – and don't forget to just breathe. That's right. Close your eyes and take a deep breath.

We were created different from men for a reason. If you put a group of men around the table, they are all eager to tell you what they bring to the table. Women, if they know their worth, well, they usually bring the table. Yes, men and women are different. However, we should be more eager to embrace that difference than spending the time trying to be equal to it. God had no intention of us being equal to man. He already knew who would bring what to the table and who would bring the table.

Let me make sure that I clarify here – I am not saying we are better than men. I am saying that God created man and then created woman (similar but different) Our differences should complement each other. Read through Genesis 2:7-25. You will see, we, man and woman, were created, given a beautiful and bountiful garden to live in. There they are, man and woman, happy, naked, not ashamed, (NO LAUNDRY to do, thanks a lot Eve! lol) then, Chapter 3- enter the serpent...

He made us similar but different. We have different talents and gifts for a reason.

To seriously grasp your worth, you must understand who you are in Christ, not who the world says you are or should be. For far too many years I let the world tell me my worth. I actually kept a running list in my Bible of things I'd been called or things I was told I could not do or accomplish. I kept the list, and get this, for the purpose of trying to better myself and not be the names and things that I was being called. HELLOOOO... How wrong is that?!

I no longer have that list. I have a new list. I shredded that old list and replaced it with what my Lord says I am to Him. When I began discovering all the beautiful things my precious Lord said I was, I began writing them down in my Bible. You see it doesn't matter what any one person, or this world says about you or me ~ it only matters what the God of the universe, the Great I AM, says about me/us.

Here are just a few of the things He says. I would encourage you to read each of these "I am" statements aloud. Before each statement either say, "I am" or your name and what is written because these are the very things the Lord is saying to me and to you, directly.

I am...
I am Blessed
I am Highly Favored
Child of the Most High God
Princess of the King of Kings
Captive of Hope
Forgiven
I am Redeemed
Pure Righteousness
I am His
I am Holy and Beloved
Restored
I am Special
A Holy Treasure
His above all Peoples in earth
I am Chosen
Called out of darkness and called into marvelous light
I am anointed
I am Lavished in His love
A delight to the Lord
Called with a Holy calling
An heir to an unshakable Kingdom
A holy temple indwelt by God
Joint heir with Christ
I am His and He is mine!

If the good Lord made sure all these things were said about you in His Word, the Holy Bible, the inerrant Word of God, then

He wanted to make sure that you knew you were special and loved.

You my dear were no mistake. You were created on purpose with a purpose for His purpose.

> *(Isaiah 43:1-3) ..." Fear not, for I have redeemed you; I have called you by your name; You are Mine. 2/ When you pass through the waters, I will be with you; And through the rivers, they shall not overflow you. When you walk through the fire, you shall not be burned, Nor shall the flame scorch you. 3/ I am the Lord your God..."*

(Isaiah 41:10) "Fear not for I am with you; Be not dismayed, for I am your God. I will strengthen you, Yes, I will help you, I will uphold you with My righteous right hand."

> *The Lord is my light and my salvation, whom shall I fear? (Psalm 27:1a)*

If these scriptures do not speak to you

and just leave you in awe and pure thankfulness, then you must have a much simpler and easier life than I do. I have walked through the fire and I need to know from where ANY strength can come from. These scriptures are full of life sustaining hope.

While you may be busy raising future Kingdom Builders, rocking a career with your super powers in the corporate world, or trying to make it through your next chemo treatment – the King Himself is busy molding you into a warrior woman. Allow Him to do His work in you.

You my dear, were handpicked and chosen by the great I am, so let's act like it.

12
FAITH ~ HOPE ~ LOVE

And now abide Faith, Hope and Love,
these three; but the greatest of these is love.

(I Corinthians 13:13)

While navigating life, you will need a couple of things; faith and hope. Oh, and let's not leave out love.

Let's start with **FAITH.** Faith is not some word that man came up with to make you feel like you are lacking in some area.

You know what I am talking about, we've all heard someone say, either to us or someone else – "If you only had faith – "You just need a little faith", etc.

Guess what? Faith is real and it was designed by God and it is a gift from God to you! (Eph. 2: 8-9) tells us this is a gift from God. He also (God through Paul) tells us in (1Cor 2:5) that our faith should not be in the wisdom of men BUT in the power of God. It just keeps getting better – it is also a shield for us!

(Eph. 6:16), "Above all, taking the shield of faith with which, you will be able to quench ALL the fiery darts of the wicked one".

Let me just stop right here and say, WOW! Who would not want a shield for that!

Many times, when the enemy sends his fiery arrows they are meant for distraction, not to kill. This is part of his strategy to throw you off your "kingdom game". Using the shield of faith will extinguish ALL of these from the wicked/evil one. Not some – ALL. This is vital my friends.

Faith is a side effect of knowing the truth, God's Truth.

Jesus Himself tells us in Matthew –

(Matthew 21:21), "Assuredly, I say to you, if you have faith and do not doubt, you will not only do what was done to the fig tree, but also if you say into the sea, 'Be removed and be cast into the sea,' it will be done.

In - (Romans 10:17) Paul tells us, *"So then faith comes by hearing, and hearing by the Word of God."*

So, I have to ask~ are you listening? Are you a true hearer of the Word? You can talk to God all day long but do you ever stop and listen?

This all goes back to- are you taking time to sit and seek Him. Are you pursuing Jesus? Are you in the Word of God? The Word of God is living and breathing, and for what you put into it you will receive much more back.

(Hebrews 11:1) tells us, "Now faith is

the substance of things hoped for, the evidence of things not seen".

If you keep reading you will see Hebrews is all about faith. The book of Hebrews tells of so many who have gone before us, and they did so with faith! It was not easy, but they had faith. They clung to faith when all else seemed overwhelming, just ask Abraham.

I believe many of us know of the scripture in (Luke 17:6) about having faith the size of a mustard seed. I could go on and on. Faith is a major player and it is a free gift from our Lord. Why would we not want it?!

I may not know much, but I do know this, I am like Paul in that I may not know a lot but this I do know, *"For I determined not to know anything among you except Jesus Christ and Him crucified.*

I say this hoping that you understand it is not I, Toni Ann Cowart, who says faith is important - but God Almighty Himself; I happen to agree with Him from my own experience. Any little thing you have gleaned from this so far - is really from the Lord.

HOPE– a feeling of confident expectation and desire for a certain thing to happen. This definition came from the dictionary.

Let me share with you what hope means to me. For me it means ~ it's not over, there's more, there's better, there's Jesus. Hope for me may not be seen but it is powerful, tangible to the heart and most powerful when gleaned from Jesus. Again, "sit & seek" and it will be given.

There are many scriptures that mention hope but my very favorite of these is from Romans.

> *(Romans 15:13), Now the God of all hope fill you with all joy and peace in believing, that you may abound in hope by the power of the Holy Spirit."*

YESSSSSS!

This right here - that He fill you with all joy and peace/you may abound in hope. With the things I have experienced in my life (sexual abuse as a child/abusive husband/divorced/burying my 6, 8, & 10 yr. old children) let me just say, I will be happy to be filled with joy and peace and abound away with hope!

We live in a world full of the good, the bad and the ugly. We are all usually okay with the "good" part, not so much with the "bad and ugly" part. This is one of the reasons hope is so vital. You see, the cross is the good, the bad and the ugly – but backwards. Bear with me here and let's look at it from a different angle.

GOOD, BAD, UGLY (vs) UGLY, BAD, GOOD

Ugly – the cross, His cross, was crudely fashioned together (nothing like the beautiful ones we hang in our homes today. It was ugly and can be viewed as much uglier when you look at the reason it was put together in the first place.

Bad – before things were over on that Friday long ago, the cross, His cross, was encrusted with blood and bits of skin must have hung where splinters pricked or dug away at His skin. The cross had become sweat soaked and blood crusted. Yes, this was bad.

Good – That wasn't the end! Oh no, that was not the end and neither was the grave that awaited His body. And that was good!

You see that was just the ending of one season before beginning a new one. The new season is full of hope.

Long, long ago on a hill called Golgotha, it turned dark and many saw it as an end, but it was really just the beginning. Yes, before that we did not have full access to God. Only the high priest could enter and even he had to make a sacrifice of himself first. It was a lot of hoopla to get to chat with God. Not anymore, and huge praises for that.

That Friday so long ago, something amazing happened. On that Friday, on a hill, there were three crosses that stood for all to see. One of those crude crosses held my Savior. That Friday it got dark, really dark...

(Matt. 27:45) "A darkness has fallen over the land... (Matt. 27:51) ...And the veil of the temple was torn in two from top to bottom; and the earth shook and the rocks were split."

We now have FULL ACCESS! No more fighting battles alone. We have full access to the One who fights for us.

(Hebrew 6:19) tells us, "this hope we have as an anchor of the soul, both sure and steadfast, and which enters the Presence behind the veil...

This is a hope I will cling to until I take my last earth side breath.

The enemy likes to come at us soft and easy at times, whispering, but once in a while, he comes at us with both barrels blazing. When he comes at us like that, then we need to be ruthless about keeping sin away and focus on Jesus.

Definition of Ruthless- having or showing no pity or compassion to others. So, why should we be any different than this towards satan?

The beauty of ruthlessness is -Jesus has allowed us full access – we are allowed face-to-face time with Him – no veil – no liaison – no commander of His army – no -no -no – FULL ACCESS. Remember, earth shook, rocks split and veil was torn to bring us face-to-face, having full access to God Himself.

We need to be souled out, intentional

and ruthless about keeping sin out so we can be focused on Him, the Great I AM.

And now abide Faith, Hope and Love, these three; but the greatest of these is love.

(I   Cor. 13:13)

LOVE, according to the dictionary is a "deep affection". I almost laugh over this definition. For any one of us who have held their firstborn knows that love is a much deeper emotion than affection, even deep affection.

Love is such a strong feeling it is very hard to describe. I believe love is our strongest emotion followed closely by grief (mainly because the deeper one loves, the deeper one grieves). Love is stronger than hate. That alone makes love very powerful.

When we love, so many things just fall into place. We are commanded to love. We are to love our God, our neighbors and our spouse.

(Deuteronomy 6:5) You shall love the Lord your God with all your heart, with all your

*soul, and with all your
strength.*

*(1 Peter 4:8) Above all things have
fervent love for one another for love will cover
a multitude of sins.*

We are to love fervently! This means
quick to forgive, even when we can't forget.
This means to go above and beyond. This
means to have a passion for others and their
needs. This mean trying our best to love
through the eyes of Jesus. When we view
people and circumstances the way Jesus
would – we can't help but love. When we
show love where others don't, people get a
glimpse of Jesus. Anytime we can let a little
Jesus shine through, then we are being a light
in a dark world.

Heaven knows our world is full of so
much hate and darkness. Why not be some
light.

*(Matthew 5:14-16) You
are the light of the world. A
city that is set on a hill cannot
be hidden. 15/ Nor do they
light a lamp and put it under a
basket, but on a lampstand,
and it gives light to all who are
in the house. 16/ Let your light*

*so shine before men, that they
may see your good works and
glorify your Father in heaven.*

In the Bible, love is the most used word.
Wow! I do believe our Lord is serious about
the whole "love" thing – we should be too.

13
YOUR STORY

There is no greater agony than bearing an untold story inside of you. ~ Maya Angelou

What is your story? What is the season you just wrapped up? Maybe your path is one you have been planning for years, or it may be one you did not ask for. Whatever your story, it is your story, and is just as unique as you are.

Our stories are ever changing, but for me, the one thing that remains the same is this – I can't share my story without the mention of my Jesus.

It is difficult to navigate life without a scratch. Many of us have ended up with a scar or two instead of a scratch. Some of us have downright reaped scars. These scars are part of what make us who we are. Some of these scars are strictly on the outside while some go very deep; so deep that others may not ever see them, but they are there.

Whatever your degree of scratches or scaring – they are yours and if you belong to Jesus then they are His too. What breaks our heart breaks His. When the enemy sees our scars, he is reminded that we survived. Yes indeed. We survived what he meant for harm. It is also a reminder to the enemy Who we belong to.

So, don't ever be ashamed of any scars you bear. Your scars are a reminder ~ you may be deeply scared, but you my dear, you are a well-seasoned warrior, who has been triumphant. A beautiful reminder. A reminder that when we are weak, He is strong.

Our stories can help others who need to know they are not alone in what they are going through. I have seen this over and over as I have shared my life and story with others. Sometimes someone just needs to know that others have walked a treacherous and tumultuous path or maybe just a similar one.

Pray and ask the Lord if it is time for you to share yours. He will guide you when the time is right.

> (2 Corinthians 1:3-4) ...God of all comfort, 4/ who comforts us in all tribulation, that we may be able to comfort those who are in any trouble, with the comfort with which we ourselves are comforted by God.

We are being transformed from soldiers, to the seasoned warriors of our stories. The enemy will always be close and ever willing to rattle our cage – Remember, and don't forget -Christ is closer.

Speaking of stories, I would like to take this opportunity and share with you a little about the incredible young woman named Tess that I dedicated this book to. This will only be a snapshot as I feel one day, she will tell her story herself to many.

Tess is beautiful, smart, sweet and has the whole world ahead of her. Tess is only 19 years old. Yet, in her short 19 years has already had reality reach out and hit her with a wicked right hook.

Picture it – Brand new graduate of High

School and you are living your "best life" during summer before College begins in the fall. It's two weeks before your 19th birthday and all seems right in your world.

It's a beautiful, sunny, and humid August day in her small Mississippi town. She slips on her tennis shoes and heads out for a run. A run she has done many times before. It was a normal day, until it wasn't.

While pounding the pavement, out of nowhere, five, yes five, pit bulls attack. They do what many predators do, they went for blood and they meant business. They did what the enemy does – they came to steal, kill and destroy. It did not matter that Tess had plans for college, nor that she is exceptionally beautiful.

No, they had their target and they were relentless. The intent was to continue to ravage until said target was no longer effective, moving, or able to make a difference in her mission. There was one problem with the enemy's attack that beautiful August day in Mississippi - the target, the victim, was underestimated and so was her God.

God already knew what would take place that day and had put things in motion. A USPS worker delivering Amazon packages, on a Sunday no less, would come upon the ongoing attack. With only what some would say was clearly the hand of God - she was able to get the dogs away and get to Tess.

Fast forward - due to the quick speed of being Life Flighted, Tess was already at the hospital in Memphis when her parents arrived. Given the Covid-19 restrictions they were not allowing her parents in with her. I cannot even begin to go into or imagine the horror that Tess had just endured, and then to find out your parents can't come in to where they are treating you. I also can't imagine from a parent's perspective of being told they could not go to her.

They weren't allowed in, until her mom went "Mississippi Mama Bear" on them- and then, mom got to go be with Tess.

The fact that Tess is alive is a miracle. There is a reason she is alive. Just listening to Tess, I already know part of that reason. While speaking with her I heard things like, "I know God has a plan... God can use this ... there must have been a reason... I will come out stronger... it will be for His Glory."

Tess went on to share with me that she had known Jesus from an early age but felt it was her freshman/sophomore year of high school that she felt she became serious about her relationship with Him. She also said that without Jesus, she has no doubt that she would have lost all hope throughout this unimaginable ordeal that she has been through.

Tess had massive injuries due to this attack. She has already had several surgeries and there will be more in her future. That August day while out for a run, was the day that her life forever changed. She is now on a journey she did not ask to take. The huge praise is she knows The One who will see her through.

Take it from those who have "been there"- lean in to Him and your story will be a whole lot sweeter. It doesn't mean bad things won't happen. It does mean you will have a peace and that you will come out on the other side of the storm. You will be able to stand where others would fall.

Tess is a beautiful example of "still standing" after literally being knocked down. There are times we must stand, so others can see Jesus. Tess is a light in a dark world. Be a light because someone else may desperately need to see that light in you. Remember, we don't know what others are dealing with.

While living out my story (which I will forever be doing) There have been a few things I have learned since I found my Jesus that I would love to share with you.

~ Rambling Remarks from a child of The King ~

Once upon a time I became His and He became mine.

At that time, I didn't fully understand what that would mean. Through time, and as layers of life have been peeled back, I've grasped an iota or two of what belonging to a Mighty God can mean.

When troubles come ~ I have a trump card.

What breaks my heart ~ breaks His

I am not alone in this thing called life.

The God who did not need me ~ He wanted me

Things will come that I do not like and some will be downright unbearable (humanly speaking- so must use trump card)

We have a choice to be an overcomer, or drown in overwhelming troubles.

When I am weak ~ He is strong

The evil one, the master manipulator, is ever stirring the pot (at least in my life) ~ BUT ~ because I belong to Jesus (unworthily so) I have not only been saved from His wrath ~ I have the ability to spread hope where satan has scattered seeds of doubt.

Thankful to be His

14
I CHALLENGE YOU

Ladies, I am leaving you with a challenge.

I challenge you to:

~ FIND OUT EXACTLY WHO GOD SAYS HE IS – don't ask someone else, dig in to His Word and ask HIM.

~ FIND OUT WHO YOU ARE IN HIM- pursue Him and you will find Him. Along the way, you will find yourself and your worth.

~ SATURATE YOURSELF WITH HIS

WORD (much of this is synonymous)

~ PRAY FOR DISCERNMENT & PREPARE FOR BATTLE!

Be a warrior for your families, and the Kingdom. Ladies, be a force to be reckoned with when satan comes a calling!

Choose Truth
Choose Obedience
Choose Jesus

If you do the above, then you have chosen to walk in faith – when you don't, then ultimately you have made a conscious decision for the opposite. That should scare you.

The Lord will not tolerate a fence straddler or someone who is luke warm. (Revelation 3:16) The Lord wants to know you are completely souled out to Him – because when you aren't, you aren't.

He tells us we can't serve two masters and basically that if we are not serving Him then we are serving the enemy. He makes Himself pretty clear in the next two passages.

(Matthew 6:24) No one can

serve two masters; for either he will hate the one and love the other, or else he will be loyal to the one and despise the other. You cannot serve God and mammon.

(1 Corinthians 10:21) You cannot drink the cup of the Lord and the cup of demons; you cannot partake of the Lord's table and of the table of demons.

In other words, find Jesus, not a religion.

Find Jesus and **FOLLOW** Jesus.

When we make things about religion instead of a relationship, we are treading on dangerous ground.

If you are willing, this would be a beautiful time to rededicate your life to Christ. He's willing and already listening.

Maybe you have never officially accepted Jesus as your Lord and Savior and instead have just been going through the motions of church. This is a perfect time to invite Him in to your heart – it's as simple as saying:

"Dear God in heaven, I admit I am a sinner and I need You and Your forgiveness. I believe that Jesus is Your one and only Son and that He died on the cross for me and my sins. I believe that You raised Him from the dead. I confess Jesus as my Lord and Savior and praise You that I am forgiven and now saved- Saved for an eternal life with my Lord in heaven."

If you just accepted Jesus for the first time ~ Welcome sweet new sister in Christ!

If you just rededicated your life to Him ~ I am sending up huge praises!

You both should know that for repentance there is joy in heaven – *Luke 15:10 "... there is joy in the presence of angels of God over one sinner who repents."*

I want you all to know that I have prayed for you and am smiling right down to my soul at the thought of your renewed spirits.

Please know that you will find your path and purpose along the way; it will not be for the weak or faint of heart. That is okay because you are special. You are set apart. You were put on this earth and in this very spot, right now – For such a time as this.

When you find yourself asking, "Now

What?", stop and take a deep breath and remember Who you belong to.

Now ladies, take up your positions on the battlefield, and remember Who fights with you.

YOUR NOTES

_____

_____

_____

_____

_____

_____

_____

_____

_____

_____

_____

_____

Now What ??

~ SCRIPTURE INDEX ~

Chapter 5 ~ Let's get Serious
Gal 1:15 NASB
Jeremiah 1:5 NASB
Matthew 11:28-29 NASB
Matthew 4:1 NASB
Luke 4:2 NKKJV
Galatians 5:7 NASB
2 Corinthians 7:10 NKJV
Colossians 3:2 NASB
Philippians 4:8 NASB
Hebrews 2:1 NKJV
Colossians 2:6-7 NKJV

Chapter 6 ~ Praying
2 Corinthians 10:3-4 NKJV
Romans 8:26 NKJV
Psalm 56:8 NKJV
Jeremiah 33:3 NKJV
Mark 1:35 NKJV
Ephesians 6:18-20 NKJV
Philippians 4:6 NKJV
James 5:13 NKJV
1 Thessalonians 5:16-18 NKJV

Chapter 7 ~ Whispers of the enemy
1 Peter 5:8 NKJV
Colossians 2:11-15 NKJV
Jeremiah 29:12-14a NKJV
John 10:10 NKJV
John 10:28 NKJV
Luke 7:43-47 NKJV

Chapter 8 ~ Shalom
John 14:27 NKJV
Psalm 29:11 NKJV
Psalm 34:14b NKJV
2 Peter 1:2 NKJV
Ephesians 1:14 NKJV
Luke 8:48 NKJV

Chapter 9 ~ Be Bold
Acts 4:13-31 NKJV
Hebrews 4:16 NKJV
Ephesians 3:12 NKJV
Proverbs 28:1 NASB
Acts 5:29 NASB
Romans 12:2 NKJV
Luke 1:37 NKJV
Luke 1 NKJV

Chapter 10 ~ Purpose
Isaiah 55:8-9 NKJV
Exodus 13:17 NKJV
Exodus 14:25 NKJV
Philippians 1:6 NASB
Luke 1:38 NKJV
James 1:2-3NKJV
Genesis 50:20 NKJV
Romans 8:28 NKJV
Deuteronomy 30:20 NKJV
James 1:5-6 NKJV
Luke 5:4-5 NKJV
Jeremiah 29:11 NKJV

Psalm 37:4 NKJV

Chapter 11 ~ Worth
Genesis 2:8 NKJV
Psalm 139:14 NKJV
Genesis 2:7-25 NKJV
Isaiah 43:1-3 NKJV
Isaiah 41:10 NKJV
Psalm 27:1a NKJV

Chapter 12 ~ Faith ~ Hope ~ Love
1 Corinthians 13:13 NKJV
Ephesians 2:8-9 NASB
Ephesians 6:16 NKJV
Romans 10:17 NKJV
Hebrews 11:1 NKJV
Romans 15:13 NASB
Matthew 27:45-51 NASB
Hebrews 6:19 NKJV
1 Corinthians 13:13 NKJV
Deuteronomy 6:5 NKJV
1 Pete 4:8 NKJV
Matthew 5:14-16 NKJV

Chapter 13 ~ Your Story
2 Corinthians 1:3-4

Chapter 14~ Challenge
Revelation 3:16 NKJV
Matthew 6:24 NKJV
1 Corinthians 10:21 NKJV

Luke 15:10 NKJV

ABOUT THE AUTHOR

Toni is a southern author who loves sharing hope with others. Toni is very passionate about her writing, speaking and digging deeper into God's Word. When there is free time, she and her husband enjoy hiking and exploring new places. She and her husband live in Huntsville, Alabama.

If you have enjoyed this book please leave a kind review on Amazon or Good Reads ~ Thank you

Connect on Social Media with Toni

Southern_and_unshackled

Toni Cowart Author

@cowartToni

Other Books by Toni Cowart

From a Mother's Heart ~ A story of Tragedy and Hope

(Non-Fiction for those hurting or grieving)

Toni also has a series of chapter books for the young readers:

The Chipmunk, the Bird and the Slithering Slimies

(Book One in The Land of Critters series)

The Bird, the Raccoon and the Skunk without a Stripe

(Book Two in The Land of Critters series)

Book three in this children's series due out soon

The Skunk Brothers, Poppy and the Dancing Trees

(Book 3 in The Land of Critters Series)

Behold, the day of the Lord is coming ~ Zechariah 14:1

Made in the USA
Columbia, SC
13 November 2020